Overview *Cacti*

Characteristics of cacti are identified discussed.

Reading Vocabulary Words

stems
spines
fruits

High-Frequency Words

home	*parts*
grow	*turn*
just	*very*
hide	*some*

Building Future Vocabulary

* These vocabulary words do not appear in this text. They are provided to develop related oral vocabulary that first appears in future texts.

Words:	*needles*	*desert*	*patterns*
Levels:	Turquoise	Library	Silver

Comprehension Strategy

Utilizing text features and structures

Fluency Skill

Pronouncing difficult words accurately

Phonics Skill

Identifying and segmenting syllables in spoken words (an-i-mals)

Reading-Writing Connection

Labeling a diagram

Send home one of the Flying Colors Take-Home books for children to share with their families.

Differentiated Instruction

Before reading the text, query children to discover their level of understanding of the comprehension strategy — Utilizing text features and structures to determine importance. As you work together, provide additional support to children who show a beginning mastery of the strategy.

Focus on ELL

- Bring in one or two real cacti. Have children gently touch the spines. Ask children to identify the stems and spines by pointing.

- Ask children where they might find cacti.

Using This Teaching Version

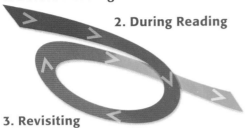

1. Before Reading
2. During Reading
3. Revisiting the Text
4. Assessment

This Teaching Version will assist you in directing children through the process of reading.

1. **Begin with Before Reading** to familiarize children with the book's content. Select the skills and strategies that meet the needs of your children.

2. **Next, go to During Reading** to help children become familiar with the text, and then to read individually on their own.

3. **Then, go back to Revisiting the Text** and select those specific activities that meet children's needs.

4. **Finally, finish with Assessment** to confirm children are ready to move forward to the next text.

1 Before Reading

Building Background

- Write *spines* on the board. Read it aloud. Ask children if they can name things with spines, such as people or cacti.

- Introduce the book by reading the title, talking about the cover photograph, and sharing the overview.

Building Future Vocabulary

Use Interactive Modeling Card: Sentence Maker

- Discuss the word *desert*. Ask *What does the* desert *look like?* (brown, dry, rocky) *How does it feel?* (hot, dry, sandy) *What kinds of animals and plants live in the* desert? (birds, lizards, spiders, cacti, scrub brush, grass)

- Have children write the word *desert* in the top box of the Sentence Maker. Have children think of phrases that make a sentence to complete the organizer.

Introduction to Reading Vocabulary

- On blank cards write: *stems*, *spines*, and *fruits*. Read them aloud. Tell children these words will appear in the text of *Cacti*.

- Use each word in a sentence for understanding.

Introduction to Comprehension Strategy

- Explain that nonfiction texts often have features and structures that help readers to better understand the text. Labels help readers understand words. Lists show important facts.

- Tell children that they will use text features and structures to help them understand important information in *Cacti*.

- Have children flip through the pages and look at some of the labels.

Introduction to Phonics

- Write the word **animal** on the board. Say the word slowly and clap with each syllable. Draw a line between syllables: an/i/mal. Point out that the word **animal** has three syllables. Tell children they can sound out segments of a difficult word to help in pronunciation of that word.

- Read aloud page 5. Have children locate the three-syllable word on the page. (**animals**)

- Have children brainstorm other three-syllable words. Say the words aloud and clap for each syllable. Write the words on chart paper.

Modeling Fluency

- Read aloud page 8, pronouncing each syllable as you read the word *beautiful*. Enunciate each syllable— beau-ti-ful. Repeat the word.

- Tell children that all readers encounter difficult words. Explain how to segment a word: look for familiar vowel sounds and consonants, say segments of the word one at a time, and then put each segment together to say the word as a whole.

2 During Reading

Book Talk
Beginning on page T4, use the During Reading notes on the left-hand side to engage children in a book talk. On page 16, follow with Individual Reading.

During Reading

Book Talk

- **Comprehension Strategy**
Explain to children that pictures and labels can help them understand the text. Ask *From looking at the photographs, what do you think these plants would feel like?* (They would feel spiny and thorny. They would hurt if you touched them.)

- Have children look at the cactus and its surroundings. Ask *Where do you think cacti grow?* (in the desert) *Do you think people eat cacti?* (maybe, if it is cooked) *What kind of animals do you think would eat cacti?* (birds) *Do you think a cactus bears fruit?* (some do, such as a prickly pear)

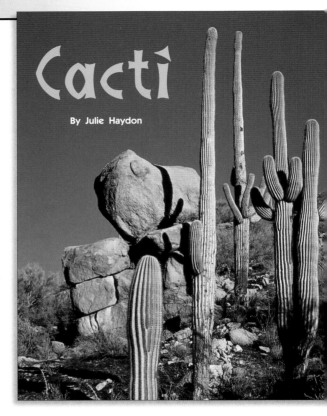

Cacti

By Julie Haydon

Turn to page 2 – Book Talk

Cacti

By Julie Haydon

Future Vocabulary

- Look at the cover photograph. Ask *Are these cacti growing in a forest or a desert?* (They are in a desert.) *How can you tell?* (A desert is rocky and dry.)

Now revisit pages 2–3

Book Talk

- Say *Look at the photographs. Do you think cacti like hot weather?* (yes) *Why or why not?*

- **Fluency Skill** Have children locate and pronounce the word *cacti* on pages 2 and 3.

- **Comprehension Strategy** Explain that labels are used to identify terms. As you point out the labels on page 2, ask *What is this label for?* (one cactus; several cacti) Point out the bulleted list on page 3. Say *Lists are used to highlight important facts. What do cacti need to grow well?* (lots of sun, air, and soil; a little water) *Does the list make the text easier to read?* (yes)

Turn to page 4 – Book Talk

This is a cactus.
A cactus is a plant.

a cactus

We say **one** cactus,
but we say **two** cacti.

cacti

2

2

Cacti need:

- lots of sun
- air
- soil
- a little water

Some cacti grow in forests, but lots of cacti grow in hot, dry places.

3

Future Vocabulary

- Have children look at the shape of the cacti. Ask *Do the cacti make patterns with their stems?* (yes) *How would you describe these patterns?* (Some cacti have a pointed pattern, and some have a folded pattern.)

Now revisit pages 4–5

During Reading

Book Talk

- **Comprehension Strategy** Ask *What labels do the illustration and photograph use?* (stem, root, and spines) *Which part of a cactus is sharp?* (spines)

- Have children locate the words *stems* and *spines* on these pages. Ask *What do cacti store in their stems?* (water) *Why do animals stay away from cacti?* (The spines are sharp and harmful.)

Turn to page 6 – Book Talk

Most cacti have thick stems and long roots.
The roots grow under the ground.

Cacti can keep water in their stems or roots for when they need it.

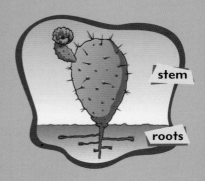

stem

roots

4

4

Can you see the spines
on this cactus?
Most cacti have spines.
The spines can be very sharp.
Most animals do not like
the sharp spines.
They keep away from cactus plants.

spines

5

Future Vocabulary

• Ask *What are needles used for?* (to sew) *How are needles similar to spines?* (Needles and spines are both sharp.) *Did you know that some trees have needles? What trees can you think of that have needles?* (Pine trees have needles instead of leaves.)

Now revisit pages 6–7

5

During Reading

Book Talk

- Ask *How tall can cacti grow?* (very tall) *How do you know?* (One cactus on this page is taller than the people.) Have children point to the tall cacti. Have them point to the round cacti.

- Ask *What does the cactus on page 7 look like?* (a nest or a ball of barbed wire) *Do the cacti on these pages have a lot of* spines? (yes)

Turn to page 8 – Book Talk

Cacti are lots of shapes and sizes. Can you see a tall cactus and some round cacti?

6

Some cacti do not look like plants at all! Look at this cactus.

7

Future Vocabulary

Future Vocabulary
- Ask children to look at page 6. Ask *What kind of patterns do you see in these cacti?* (The round cacti have a ball pattern. Their spines have a circular pattern. In the tall cactus, the spines go up and down the stem.) Encourage children to tell about other patterns they see in nature.

Now revisit pages 8–9

During Reading

Book Talk

- **Comprehension Strategy** Ask *How do these labels help the reader?* (The reader can see what cactus flowers and cactus fruits look like.)
  Did you know that cacti had flowers? Do cactus flowers have a smell? (Some do.)
  What happens to the cactus flowers? (They turn into fruits.)

- **Phonics Skill** Have children locate the words *flowers* and *beautiful* on page 8. Remind children to break difficult words into segments so they can pronounce them.

- **Fluency Skill** Have children read aloud the sentence that includes the words *flowers* and *beautiful*.

Turn to page 10 – Book Talk

Cacti grow flowers.
Cactus flowers can be very big and very beautiful.
Some cactus flowers
have a very strong smell.

cactus flowers

8

8

The flowers turn into fruits.
Some cactus fruits are red
or yellow or white
and look like berries.

cactus
fruits

9

Future Vocabulary

- Ask *Do you think of flowers when you think about the desert? Why or why not?* (Probably not; the desert is dry and sandy.)

- Ask *What fruits are you familiar with?* (apples, bananas, oranges) *Do you think fruits would grow well in the desert?* (No, the desert is dry.)

Now revisit pages 10–11

During Reading

Book Talk

- Ask *What is inside the fruit?* (seeds) *What happens to the seeds?* (Some fall to the ground, and new cacti grow from them.)

- Ask *What happens to the fruits?* (The birds eat some. Some fall and rot on the ground.) *Do you think a bird can get hurt by the spines?* (Yes, if it is not careful and it touches the spines.)

Turn to page 12 – Book Talk

There are seeds inside the fruits.

Some of the fruits open,
and the seeds fall out.

Some of the fruits are eaten
by birds and animals.
The birds and animals
drop the seeds.

10

10

Some of the fruits
fall to the ground and rot.
The seeds are washed away by rain.

New cacti grow from the seeds.

11

Future Vocabulary
• Ask children to study the picture on page 10. Ask *Do the spines have a* pattern? *What kind of* pattern? (The spines have a straight pattern. They are in a straight line.)

Now revisit pages 14–15

During Reading

Book Talk

- Remind children that birds eat the fruits of cacti. Ask *What other part of the cacti do birds eat?* (parts of the flowers)

- **Comprehension Strategy** Ask *How does the label on page 13 help the reader?* (Without the label, the reader might not know those are insects.) *Why do you think people would want to cook the stems before eating them?* (to get rid of the insects)

Turn to page 14 – Book Talk

Some animals eat cacti.
Some animals live in cacti.

Insects, bats, and birds
eat parts of the flowers.

12

These insects eat the stems.

Some people eat the stems, too.
They cook the stems first.

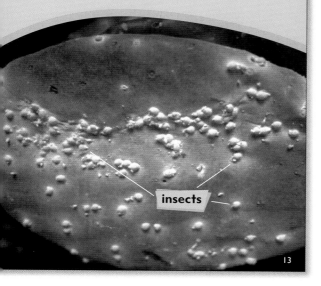

insects

13

During Reading

Book Talk

- Say *In some places, cacti are grown as a crop, or food plant. What other plants are grown as food?* (wheat, corn, apples) *Do you think growing cacti would be difficult?* (Yes, because they have spines. No, because they do not need a lot of water.)

- **Phonics Skill** Have children say the word *people* aloud. Clap out the syllables together. Have children find other words on page 14 with two syllables. *(cacti, places)*

Turn to page 16 – Book Talk

Some people eat the fruits. In some places, people grow cacti for the fruits and stems.

Revisiting the Text

Birds and rats make nests in cacti.
Snakes hide under cacti.

15

Future Vocabulary

- Have children reread page 14. Ask them to think about what kind of places are good for growing cacti. (deserts, dry places)

- Say *The book says that cacti live in hot, dry places. Does this place look dry? Do you think it is a* desert*?* (yes) *How can you tell?* (There are no big trees in the picture. The big rock looks like it belongs in the desert.)

- Talk about what kind of animals live in the desert. Ask *How do cacti help* desert *animals?* (Desert animals eat cacti and make nests in cacti.)

Go to page T5 —
   Revisiting the Text

15

During Reading

Book Talk
- Leave this page for children to discover on their own when they read the book individually.

Individual Reading
Have each child read the entire book at his or her own pace while remaining in the group.

Go to page T5 – Revisiting the Text

Some people just like to look at cacti.
They grow cacti at home for fun. You can, too!

16

During independent work time, children can read the online book at:
www.rigbyflyingcolors.com

Revisiting the Text

Future Vocabulary

- Use the notes on the right-hand pages to develop oral vocabulary that goes beyond the text. These vocabulary words first appear in future texts. These words are: *needles*, *desert*, and *patterns*.

Turn back to page 1

Reading Vocabulary Review
Activity Sheet: Word Rater

- Have children write *stems* in the word box. Then have them circle the statement that best describes their knowledge of the word.

- Have children write any associations they have for the word *stems*.

- Give children each a dictionary in which to look up the word. Tell them to copy the definition and write a sentence using the word.

Comprehension Strategy Review
Use Interactive Modeling Card: Summarizing

- Read aloud a page of text and model summarizing it.

- Write in the book's page numbers, and work with children to summarize each page spread in one or two sentences.

Phonics Review

- Have children look for words with more than one syllable. *(cactus, cacti, forests, places, water, animals, flowers, beautiful, inside, insects, people)*

- Have children divide three-syllable words in a three-column chart. Have them practice saying the words aloud segment by segment, slowly at first, then faster each time through.

Fluency Review

- Turn to page 10 and have children take turns reading the sentences aloud to a partner.

- Remind them how to divide words into syllables. Listen to partners and make sure each child is correctly pronouncing words such as *inside, open, eaten,* and *animals.*

Reading-Writing Connection
Activity Sheet: Questions and Answers Chart

To assist children with linking reading and writing:

- Help children complete the Questions and Answers Chart.

- Have children use the answers in their charts to label a simple diagram of a cactus.

Assessing Future Vocabulary

Work with each child individually. Ask questions that elicit each child's understanding of the Future Vocabulary words. Note each child's responses:

- What kind of plants are suited for the desert: plants that need a lot of water or plants that need little water? Why?
- What kinds of plants have needles?
- What kind of patterns do the spines of cacti have?

Assessing Comprehension Strategy

Work with each child individually. Note each child's understanding of text features and text structures:

- What is a label?
- How do labels help readers?
- What is a list?
- How do lists help readers?
- Was each child able to explain the importance of text features and text structures?

Assessing Phonics

Work with each child individually. Provide the note cards with three-syllable words that the children brainstormed earlier in the lesson. Ask each child to look at the word and say it aloud. Note each child's responses for understanding syllables:

- Did each child divide each word into syllables?
- Did each child pronounce each syllable in each word?
- Did each child say each word as a unit?

Assessing Fluency

Have each child individually read page 14 to you. Note each child's understanding of accurately pronouncing difficult words:

- Was each child able to pronounce segments of a word?
- Was each child able to correctly pronounce the two- and three-syllable words?

Interactive Modeling Cards

Sentence Maker

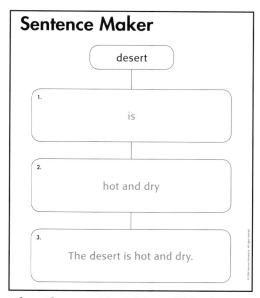

desert

1. is

2. hot and dry

3. The desert is hot and dry.

Directions: With children, fill in the Sentence Maker using the word *desert*.

Summarizing

Page	Summary
2–3	Cacti are plants. They need lots of sun to grow.
4–5	Cacti have stems that store water. Cacti have sharp spines.
6–7	Cacti come in many shapes and sizes.
8–9	Cacti have beautiful flowers. The flowers turn into fruits.
10–11	Birds and animals eat the seeds. New cacti come from seeds.
12–13	Animals and people eat stems. People cook the stems.
14–15	People grow cacti for food. Birds make nests in cacti.
16	Growing cacti is fun.

Directions: With children, fill in the Summarizing table for *Cacti*.

Discussion Questions

- What do cacti need to grow well? (Literal)
- How do the stems help the cacti survive? How do the spines help protect the cacti? (Critical Thinking)
- Why would people eat cacti? (Inferential)

Activity Sheets

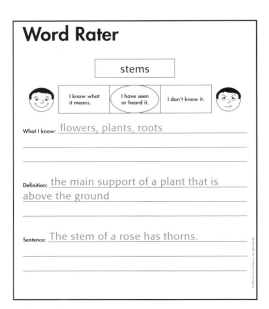

Word Rater

stems

| | I know what it means. | I have seen or heard it. | I don't know it. | |

What I know: flowers, plants, roots

Definition: the main support of a plant that is above the ground

Sentence: The stem of a rose has thorns.

Directions: Have children fill in the Word Rater using the word *stems*. Then have children write associations for it, define it, and write a sentence with the word *stems*.

Questions and Answers Chart

Title Cacti
Topic Cacti

Questions	Answers
What is a cactus?	It is a plant with spines.
Where do cacti grow?	They grow in hot, dry places.
What do cacti look like?	Some are tall and skinny. Others are short and round. They have spines.
Do cacti bloom?	Yes, they have flowers that turn into fruit.
Can people eat the fruit?	Yes, people eat the fruits and stems.
How do people prepare cacti to eat?	They cook the stems.

Directions: Have children fill in the Questions and Answers Chart for *Cacti*. Optional: Have children use information from the chart to draw and label a diagram of a cactus.